FOR BEGINNERS INVESTING CRYPTOCURRENCY

An Absolute Beginners Guide to Learn About Cryptocurrency, Bitcoin, and Blockchain Technology From Scratch to Become Successful and Make Handsome Profits

Amy Satpalson

Hardcover ISBN: 978-93-95862-98-1
Paperback ISBN: 978-93-95862-97-4
eBook ISBN: 978-93-95862-88-2

©Publisher

Publisher: Pharos Books (P) Ltd.
Plot No.-55, Main Mother Dairy Road
Pandav Nagar, East Delhi-110092
Phone: 011-40395855, +4049916623
WhatsApp: +91 8368220032
E-mail: sales@pharosbooks.in
Website: www.pharosbooks.in
First Edition: 2023

Printed By: Sushma Book Binding House, Okhla
Industrial Area, Phase II, New Delhi-110020

Cryptocurrency Investing for Beginners
By Amy Satpalson

CONTENTS

Introduction

So you've picked up this book, and your first thought is, undoubtedly, "What the hell is a cryptocurrency?" To put it simply, cryptocurrency is a new type of digital cash. You can digitally transfer traditional, non-cryptocurrency money like the US dollar, but this isn't the same as how cryptocurrencies function. When cryptocurrencies become more ubiquitous, you may be able to use them to make electronic purchases like you would with traditional currencies. On the other hand, cryptocurrencies are distinguished by the technology that underpins them. "Who cares about the technology underlying my money?" you could ask. Do you realize how your daily, government-issued cash is held in banks? And that you'll need an ATM or a bank link to obtain more or transfer it to others? If you are a bitcoins user, you might be able to do away with banks and other centralized intermediaries entirely. This is because cryptocurrencies rely on a decentralized technology called blockchain (meaning no single entity is in charge of it).

Before delving into the specifics of cryptocurrencies, it's important first to grasp the notion of money. Money philosophy is similar to "which came first: the chicken or the egg?" Money must possess several properties to be valuable. Enough people must own it, merchants must accept it as a form of payment, and society must have faith that it is worthwhile and will continue to be important in the future. Of all, when you sold your chicken for shoes back in the day, the swapped commodities' worth was inherent. However, the meaning of money and, more crucially, the trust model of money altered when coins, cash, and credit cards were introduced. Another significant difference in money is the ease with which it may be transferred. One of the key reasons for the invention of currency was the difficulty of transporting a tonne of gold bars from one country to another. Then came credit cards, which were developed as people became lazier. On the other hand, credit cards transport money that your government controls. Cryptocurrencies may provide a helpful alternative as the globe grows more linked and individuals become more concerned about authorities who may or may not be acting in their best interests.

CHAPTER 1

What is Currency —An Overview

The physical money in an economy is currency, consisting of coins and paper notes in circulation. Currency accounts for a minor portion of the total money supply, which is largely made up of credit money or computerized entries in financial ledgers. Most of the transactions we engage in daily involve currency, whether we use paper bills or swipe a credit card. Money is, without a doubt, the lifeblood of economies all across the world. Paper money and coins in circulation are referred to as currency. However, the currency is only a minor part of the monetary system and is only one factor to consider when calculating the overall money supply. Indeed, most money today is credit money or electronic records maintained in a bank or financial institution system. Unlike early currency, which was backed wholly by social agreement and faith in the issuer, today's fiat money is backed entirely by social agreement and faith in the issuer. For traders, currencies are the units of account of different nations/states that exchange values fluctuate.

1.1 What is Currency?

While the specific meaning of money may appear evident because we all utilize it daily, it may also be mysterious and subtle. Assume you work as a shoemaker and need to buy a loaf of bread to feed your family. You approach the baker and make a deal for a specified quantity of loaves in exchange for a pair of shoes. But, as it turns out, he doesn't need shoes right now. Or you can find another baker nearby who is also short on shoes, or you're out of luck. Money, according to conventional economics, solves this problem. It functions as a universal store of value that other members of society can access. Instead of shoes, that same baker might want a table. Transactions might move faster in general since sellers have an easier time finding a buyer with whom they wish to do business. Most crucially, money must be the unit of account, or numeraire, which is a fancy term for the unit where goods in a community are priced. That is the dollar in the United States. People can exchange credit without using physical money after a unit of account has been established.

A merchant that accepts the currency can sell their items while also having a handy way to pay their trading partners. Currency has several additional essential advantages. Coins and dollar bills are easy to travel due to their small size. Consider a corn farmer who had to fill a cart with groceries every time he needed to buy something.

Furthermore, coins and paper benefit from lasting for a long period, which is not true for all goods. For example, a farmer who relies on direct trade might only have a few weeks before his assets perish. He may accumulate and store the wealth with money.

1.2 Various Forms of Currency That Existed in Different Periods

It's normal to equate money with coins or paper bills nowadays. On the other hand, the currency has assumed various forms throughout history. Certain commodities became a traditional method of payment in many early communities. Instead of bartering items directly, the Aztecs frequently used cocoa beans. Commodities, on the other hand, have evident disadvantages in this sense. Depending on their size, they can be difficult to transport from one location to another. They also have a limited shelf life in many situations. These are only a few reasons why coined currency was such a significant development. Egyptians made metal rings that were used as money as early as 2500 B.C., while real coins have been available since at least 700 B.C., when a population utilized them in Turkey. The Tang Dynasty in China, which lasted from 618 to 907 A.D., was the first to use paper money. Since the dawn of civilization, metallic money, such as coins composed of precious metals like gold, silver, or copper, has been used. Large circular stones in the Pacific Islands, cowrie shells in pre-modern America, tobacco leaves, grain and salt measurements, or even cigarettes and packets of ramen noodles in jails have all been used as types of currency. Technology has just permitted a completely new type of payment: electronic cash. Western Union performed the first electronic money transfer in 1871, using a telegraph network. With the introduction of mainframe computers, banks could debit or credit each other's accounts without having to move significant sums of money physically. Electronic payments and digital money are now not only prevalent but also the most essential and widely used types of payment.

1.3 Value in Currency

So, what gives our modern currencies their worth, whether it's an American dollar or a Japanese yen? Unlike early coins made of precious metals, most modern coins have little intrinsic value. It keeps its value, though, for one of two reasons. To begin with, "representative money" allows each coin or note to be exchanged for a specific amount of a commodity. In the years after WWII, when central banks worldwide could pay the US government $35 for an ounce of gold, the dollar fell into this group.

To put it in another way, the paper money was a claim on physical metal that could be legally redeemed for it on demand. However, President Nixon canceled the deal with governments worldwide due to concerns about a possible run on America's gold supply. The dollar became fiat money after completely separated from the gold standard. In other words, it has value simply because individuals trust that others will accept it. Most of the world's main currencies, including the euro, the British pound, and the Japanese yen, now fall into this group. Furthermore, the value of fiat money is derived from public trust in the government's ability to levy and collect taxes.

1.4 Exchange-Rate and Financial Markets

While currency refers to real money, financial markets refer to currencies as the units of account and cross-currency exchange rates of national economies. Due to the global nature of trade, parties regularly need to obtain foreign currency. Governments have two basic policy options when it comes to controlling this process. The first alternative is to give an exchange rate that is predetermined. The government sets the exchange rate between the two denominations by pegging its currency to a major foreign currency like the US dollar or the euro. To keep the local exchange rate stable, a country's central bank either buys or sells the currency it is tied to. The primary goal of a fixed exchange rate is to provide a sense of stability, which is especially crucial when a country's financial markets are less sophisticated than those in other parts of the world. When investors know how much of the pegged currency they can buy if they want to, they gain confidence.

On the other hand, fixed exchange rates have been implicated in several previous currency crises. This can happen when the central bank buys a local currency, resulting in an overvaluation. An alternative to this strategy is to let the money float. The market sets the value of foreign currency rather than the government fixing it ahead of time. Several significant economies employ a floating exchange rate, notably the United States. In a floating system, supply and demand laws govern the price of a foreign currency. As a result, the denomination gets less expensive for overseas investors as the quantity of money grows. Growth in demand will also help the currency gain traction (make it more expensive). While having a "strong" currency offers benefits, it also has drawbacks. For example, suppose the dollar has grown in value against the yen. Japanese companies will be forced to pay a higher price for American-made goods, which they will almost definitely pass on to customers. As a result, American products in overseas markets are less competitive.

1.5 Inflation and Its Impact

Today, fiat currencies are used by most of the world's major economies. Because they are not tied to any tangible object, governments have the freedom to create additional money in times of financial difficulty. While having more alternatives for dealing with difficulties provides you with more options, it also allows you to overpay. The most significant danger of producing too much money is hyperinflation. As more money is circulated, each unit of cash loses its value. While small quantities of inflation have minimal influence on a country's economy, unrestrained devaluation has the potential to erode consumers' purchasing power drastically. If yearly inflation exceeds 5%, each person's funds will be worth 5% less than the previous year, providing no significant interest is made. Maintaining the same standard of life becomes increasingly

                                    Cryptocurrency Investing For Beginners

challenging. As a result, central banks in wealthy nations often strive to keep inflation in check by withdrawing money from circulation indirectly when the currency loses too much value.

Crux

Regardless of the form, all currencies have the same essential purposes. It stimulates economic activity by broadening the market for a wide range of goods. It also enables customers to preserve money and satisfy long-term requirements. Money is used to be restricted to tangible coins and banknotes, but in today's digital economy, money is now held as data in bank ledgers. It is even surpassing the idea of tangibility with the introduction of cryptocurrencies like Bitcoin, which can never be made physical.

CHAPTER **2**

Journey From Fiat Money to Cryptocurrency

Cryptocurrency is a new type of currency protected by cryptography, a type of electronic encryption that makes counterfeiting impossible. The growth of cryptocurrencies has sparked a debate over the future of fiat money, such as the US Dollar or the UK Pound, which the government backs. Though virtual currency is growing in popularity, it is still not able to completely replace fiat currency, which is still the most widely used method of exchanging value around the world. Given their volatile nature, most people regard cryptocurrencies as a means of rapidly accumulating wealth. Let us first go through the history of fiat money and then move on to the advent and rise of cryptocurrency.

                   Cryptocurrency Investing For Beginners

2.1 History of Money

Money has always been in use by humans throughout history in some form or another for at least 5,000 years. Bartering was probably used earlier in that era, according to historians. For example, a farmer may exchange a bushel of wheat for a pair of shoes from a shoemaker.

2.1.1 How Did the World Transition From Barter to the Currency System?

On the other hand, the arrangement mentioned above requires time. If you're trading an ax as part of an arrangement in which the other party is obligated to kill a woolly mammoth, you'll need to find someone who thinks an ax is a fair trade for facing down a woolly mammoth's 12-foot tusks. If that doesn't work, you'll have to alter the agreement's terms until someone agrees. Over time, a currency based on readily transferred products such as animal skins, salt, and swords developed. The products that were exchanged were utilized as a type of money. In many situations, however, the worth of each of these commodities was up to discussion. This global trade system evolved and is still used in some regions today. One of the most significant accomplishments of the introduction of money was the rapidity with which commerce could be done, whether mammoth-slaying or monument-building. In early August 2021, Chinese archaeologists from Zhengzhou's State University announced that they had discovered the world's earliest known, securely dated currency minting operation. A mint is a facility that produces money. Around 640 BCE, this facility at Guanzhuang, Henan Province, China, began striking spade coins, which are thought to be the first standardized metal currency.

2.1.2 Origin of Coin Minting

Meanwhile, the Lydians were credited with the invention of metal money by the sixth-century BCE. Lydia's King Alyattes minted the Lydian stater, which is said to be the first official currency around 600 BCE. The coins were made of electrum, a naturally occurring mixture of silver and gold, and were embossed with images that served as denominations. A clay jar may cost you two owls and a snake in the streets of Sardis around 600 BCE. Lydia's money aided the country's internal and external trading systems, allowing it to become one of Asia Minor's wealthiest empires. "As rich as Croesus," as the phrase goes now, refers to the last Lydian monarch who created the first gold coin.

2.1.3 When the World Transitioned to Paper Currency

Around 700 CE, the Chinese moved from coins to paper money. By the time Marco Polo—a Venetian trader, adventurer, and writer who traveled through Asia along the Silk Road between 1271 and 1295 CE—visited China in around 1271 CE, the emperor of China had a firm grip on both the money supply and its multiple denominations. Where the words "In God We Trust" currently appear on modern American dollars, a Chinese inscription at the time threatened to decapitate counterfeiters. Metal coins were the sole form of money in several regions of Europe until the 16th century. New sources of precious metals were given by colonial conquests, allowing European powers to continue minting a larger quantity of coins. Meanwhile, banks began issuing paper banknotes to depositors and borrowers in place of metal coins. These notes may be presented to the bank and exchanged for metal coins for their face value (usually silver or gold). This paper money can be exchanged for goods and services. It functioned similarly to cash in today's society in this sense. However, instead of the government, which is today in charge of money in most nations, it was issued by banks and private companies. The colonial rulers of North America issued the first paper money created by a European country. Because transportation between Europe and the North American colonies was slow, the colonies occasionally ran out of money. Instead of returning to barter, colonial administrations issued IOUs used as money. This happened for the first time in Canada, which was still a French colony. In 1685, soldiers gave playing cards worth French coins signed by the governor and could be used as payment instead of French coins.

2.2 Theories Behind the Creation of Money

There are three major theories about the origin of money:

2.2.1 Money Was Created for Trading Purposes

Most economists believe that money evolved because it was more flexible than bartering for trade purposes. This meant that currency was a precious asset, such as cattle in ancient civilizations, gold and silver by weight later, and gold and silver coins eventually. All this sounds fair enough when you know that it is an attempt to explain the roots of metallic currency; otherwise, cattle don't fall into this definition of metallic money. Moreover, a high degree of growth would be expected through metallic money: it would suggest an acknowledgment of private property in contrast to tribal property, and it would imply recognition of contracts and compliance by a legal structure. At the same time, cattle are much easier to be recognized as money since it is easy for a primitive culture to value, to impose a value without a legal structure unilaterally.

2.2.2 Money Was Created for Social Purposes

The second theory says the money was created for social reasons, such as fixing a bride's price and blood money for someone killed or wounded by another tribe.

2.2.3 Money Was Created for Religious Purposes

The third theory says that money was created for religious purposes. In his book Holy Gold, Bernard Laum notes that the root of money was in the Eastern temples, and it was used as the mandated sacrifice to the gods and for the priests' payment.

 Cryptocurrency Investing For Beginners

2.3 Currency Wars

The adoption of paper money in Europe expanded the number of international trade possibilities. The first currency market was established when banks and the ruling classes began purchasing currencies from other countries. The value of a country's currency, and hence its capacity to trade on an increasingly worldwide market, was influenced by the stability of a monarchy or government. Competition between countries frequently resulted in currency wars, in which competing nations attempted to modify the value of the enemy's currency by boosting it and making the enemy's goods too expensive, reducing it and lowering the enemy's purchasing power (and ability to pay for a war), or eliminating the currency.

2.4 Mobile Payments

Mobile payments and virtual currency are two new types of currency that have emerged in the twenty-first century. Mobile payments are made using a portable electronic device such as a cellphone, smartphone, or tablet to pay for a product or service. Money can be sent to friends and family members via mobile payment technologies. Apple Pay and Google Pay are increasingly competing for businesses to use their platforms for point-of-sale payments.

2.5 Virtual Currency

The pseudonymous Satoshi Nakamoto released Bitcoin in 2009, and it swiftly became the de facto standard for virtual currency. Virtual currencies have no physical coinage, and as of November 2021, all of the world's bitcoin was valued at a little over $1 trillion, or about 3% of all of the world's money. The attractiveness of virtual money is that it promises reduced transaction fees compared to traditional online payment channels and, unlike government-issued currencies, is managed by a decentralized authority.

The Bottom Line

Money's history is still being written. From trading animal skins to minting coins to printing paper money, we appear to be on the verge of a dramatic shift to electronic transactions and cryptocurrencies like Bitcoin. Bartering still exists on the margins in some industries, such as the business-to-business (B2B) space and some consumer services, as evidence of how ancient transaction forms have been co-opted. As long as humans require a medium of exchange, the monetary system will undoubtedly evolve.

2.6 Origin of Cryptocurrency

Now we will discuss the origin of cryptocurrency and its unprecedented popularity as a medium of exchange.

2.6.1 What is Digital Money?

Any form of money or payment that occurs only in electronic form is digital money or digital currency. A tangible type, such as a bill, receipt, or coins, is missing in digital currency. In machines, it is accounted for and transmitted using electronic codes. Payments are becoming more automated as automation becomes more popular, culminating in less need for tangible money. New types of technology now allow digital money to be used more safely and effortlessly. With technology such as credit cards, smartphones, and online crypto-currency transactions, digital money can be transferred and traded. This is cryptography-secured digital money, which makes it even harder to counterfeit or double-spend. It operates through decentralized blockchain technology-based networks, a database stored through a computing network. Cryptocurrencies are not distributed by a central bank or government, which frees them from the impediment of government interference or abuse.

2.6.2 History of Digital Money

Digital money's history dates back to the internet's inception. In the early days, there were challenges in getting the community to support digital currency; but as people get more familiar with technology and the technology itself gets simpler and safer, more people are now eager to use digital money. PayPal is considered one of the first popular enterprises to introduce the concept of easy-to-use automated financial transactions to mass adoption.

2.7 History of Cryptocurrency

The cryptocurrency world has progressed leaps and bounds around the globe since the advent of Bitcoin in 2009. What originated as an unproven idea is now regarded by many as the currency's future. Thousands of other cryptocurrencies have joined Bitcoin since the opening of the crypto exchange, including the following:

- Ethereum
- XRP
- Tether
- Bitcoin Cash
- Litecoin
- EOS

2.8 What is Cryptocurrency?

To understand how digital currency has become so popular, it is important to understand what digital currency is. Cryptocurrencies decentralize currencies in very basic words so that the government does not regulate the money. However, it becomes a challenge to check transfers without a single agency and stop double-spending. That is when the culture of cryptographers comes into play. Cryptocurrency transactions are effectively distributed to the whole network through cryptography and blockchain, rather than checking a transaction via a centralized third party. This public ledger tracks all transactions in an open-source network, empowering anyone to see transactions. Transactions are only done when cryptocurrency miners validate the transaction by solving a cryptographic puzzle. In cryptocurrencies, by legitimizing transfers, miners operate as a third party, close to the government in regular currency transactions. Crypto miners are, however, paid with crypto from the network itself instead of taking a share of the trade and the money of the participants. To preserve the integrity of the transaction history, this system encourages everybody in the blockchain. This solution to the conventional financial system has become more and more attractive as it encourages individuals without a watchful third eye to have more power over their money. Now, let's look back at the monumental steps of a cryptocurrency over the past 10-plus years.

2.9 The Timeline of Cryptocurrency

Given below is a chronological timeline of cryptocurrency.

2.9.1 Initial Failure

Although cryptocurrencies were not legally mined until 2009, there were other attempts to set up a digital currency in previous years. In 1998, two founders of cryptocurrencies, Wei Dai and Nick Szabo, published ideas on the prospect of currency decentralization. Both of their proposals revolved around digital currencies to replace conventional financial system inefficiencies, such as spending money on paper and coin currency formation. Although no proposal came to fruition, Dai and Szabo became early cryptocurrency adapters more than a decade later. The first true cryptocurrency, Bitcoin creation, resulted from these initial failures.

2.9.2 October 2008

The world of cryptocurrency started when a white paper Bitcoin was published by a person or group of people: a Peer-to-Peer Electronic Cash System under the pseudonym of Satoshi Nakamoto. This publication explained what Bitcoin is and why it is equivalent to conventional financial schemes. Introducing the blockchain to the world appeared to fix the missing piece in digital currencies for the first time. The paper by Nakamoto followed up on some of the early concepts that struggled to appear a decade ago and became, as we know it, the base for cryptocurrencies.

2.10 Bitcoin Timeline

2.10.1 January 2009

Less than three months later, by mining the first block of Bitcoin, Nakamoto announced the official beginning of the crypto-currency universe. Nakamoto was given 50 Bitcoins for approving the first transaction, the beneficiary of which was Hal Finney, called the Genesis Block of Bitcoin. The momentum for the digital currency was formally underway, with transactions officially registered and the Bitcoin network legitimized.

2.10.2 March 2010

More than a year after official trade, the first cryptocurrency trading market was introduced in the form of the now-discontinued BitcoinMarket.com. On a Bitcoin forum, a consumer who wanted to begin treating Bitcoin as a currency that people might share and exchange for dollars suggested this groundbreaking growth. Traders could potentially gauge the worth of a single Bitcoin, priced initially at fractions of a penny.

2.10.3 May 2010

Laszlo Hanyecz reported the first purchase of products using Bitcoin with the first digital currency trading market set up and rising at an encouraging pace. Hanyecz bought two Papa John's pizzas for 10,000 Bitcoin on May 22, 2010, estimated at $80 million in 2018. The validity of the cryptocurrency has further solidified this day. It has since then been annually celebrated as Bitcoin Pizza Day.

2.10.4 February— June 2011

At this point, when other trading markets took center stage, including the notorious Mt. Gox market, BitcoinMarket. com was becoming more irrelevant. February marked the first time that Bitcoin hit parity with the US dollar as its value began to soar. Throughout the year, competing cryptocurrencies have also started to emerge. When hackers stole 2,000 Bitcoins in June, the first cryptocurrency attack occurred on Mt. Gox. The market continued to rise in notoriety and holdings amid the hack.

2.10.5 The Year 2013

Two years fast forward, and Mt. Gox is easily the world's biggest currency market. According to Investopedia, the market accounted for more than 70 percent of all Bitcoin trades at its peak in 2013. Although excitement soared, the exchange's extreme notoriety still gave hackers a golden chance.

2.10.6 February 2014

Mt. Gox went from being the biggest Bitcoin exchange globally to bankrupt in the space of a month. The exchange was the victim of the most important hack in the history of cryptocurrencies. Hackers looted from Mt. Gox consumers an astronomical 744,408 Bitcoins and an additional 100,000 from the exchange itself. The valuation was $460 million at the time.

Consequently, the hack forced Bitcoin's worth to nosedive by 50% in the coming months. Although the value of the cryptocurrency subsequently returned to its pre-attack metrics, the hack itself highlighted the need for more robust security measures.

2.10.7 July 2015

As Bitcoin and rival cryptocurrencies were still recovering from the hack's shock, a new cryptocurrency was introduced, carrying another degree of protection. The Ethereum network was established to exchange the ether cryptocurrency as a platform. The network made the use of smart contracts, a common cryptographic software that makes it much easier to promote credible transactions without a third party at all being present. The Ethereum network, along with its smart contracts, is now used by multiple cryptocurrencies in the form of ERC-20 tokens in the world of cryptocurrencies. ERC-20 tokens vary because they are assets generated by the smart contracts of the Ethereum network. In contrast, Bitcoin and other crypto coins have their blockchain and thus coexist with the blockchain of Ethereum.

2.10.8 Present Value of Cryptocurrency Market

The value of the cryptocurrency market has surpassed $3 trillion. Since investors have become more acquainted with established tokens like Bitcoin while networks like Ethereum and Solana continue to develop and attract additional features, the market for digital assets has approximately doubled from its 2020 year-end value. The interest in non-fungible tokens and decentralized finance is expanding, and meme coins like Dogecoin and Shiba Inu continue to draw attention.

2.11 Difference Between Cryptocurrency and Fiat Money

Unlike conventional money, cryptocurrency is neither governed nor supported by governments. As a result, the virtual currency lacks the same level of trustworthiness as the real thing (hard cash or digital money in bank accounts). Furthermore, cryptocurrencies are significantly more volatile than traditional cash. The volatility is partly due to the transaction's speculative nature, in which participants are intent on quickly gaining money by recording gains. Cryptocurrencies, unlike conventional money, do not require an intermediary to authenticate a transaction. To validate crypto transactions, blockchain technology is employed, which means that all trading activities are permanently recorded, enhancing the security of any exchange.

2.12 Similarities Between Currency Notes and Cryptocurrency

Both of these types of currency get much of their value from their widespread adoption worldwide. Moreover, increased public acceptance of either of the two currencies results in increased credibility in the financial world. They're also divisible, as Bitcoin can be divided into 0.00000001 BTC. Cryptocurrencies, like fiat money, could be used to pay for services and purchase goods. They could also be offered as a gift that serves as a value store.

2.13 Differences Between Physical Money, Digital Money, and Cryptocurrency

Explained below are the critical features of each type of money.

2.13.1 Physical Money

Traditional currency is the money that a country's Financial Authority issues, and it is assessed as currency plus deposits at the central bank by banks and other institutions. It is also the type of money that can meet the commercial banks' reserve requirements.

2.13.2 Digital Money

Digital money (electronic currency or electronic money) is a currency that is only available in digital form and not in physical form (such as banknotes and coins). It exhibits physical currency-like properties but enables immediate transfers and borderless transfer-of-ownership.

Concepts such as cryptocurrency, digital currency, and Bitcoin have become big buzzwords as money becomes more digitized in the payments world. In the later part of this chapter, we will explore how it varies from standard modes of payment, including cash, credit, and debit cards.

2.13.3 Cryptocurrency

Bitcoin, often referred to as digital money, is a virtual currency that can be sent/received digitally. The digital currency reflects a value not provided by any country or government by a financial body. Still, individuals adopt it as a form of payment for goods or services. There are over 900 cryptocurrencies available on the internet, and it is possible to build new cryptocurrencies at any time. Bitcoin, Ripple, and Ethereum are three of the bigger players you may have heard of.

CHAPTER **3**

Cryptocurrency and Blockchain

Cryptocurrency is sometimes referred to as the Unicorn of the Twenty-First Century or as "future riches." A cryptocurrency is a digital money with very few entries in a ledger that no one can change. These entries can't be changed unless they meet specific criteria. This may seem mundane, but believe it or not, this is the correct way to describe cryptocurrencies. Consider the money in your bank account. Are there more than database records that can only be changed under specific circumstances? It is also possible to take genuine coins and banknotes. What are they, if not limited, entries that can only be updated if the situation is documented in a public physical record rather than if the notes and coins are physically owned? Money is all about a verifiable entry in any ledger of deposits, balances, and transfers. Cryptocurrency is an internet-based exchange mechanism that executes financial transactions using cryptographic processes. It uses blockchain technology to promote decentralization, openness, and immutability. The most important feature of a cryptocurrency is that any central government does not regulate it. Because of the decentralized nature of the blockchain, cryptocurrencies may be resistant to traditional forms of government regulation and interference. Cryptocurrencies may be traded directly between two parties using private and public keys. These transactions may be completed with low transaction costs, allowing users to avoid paying hefty fees to traditional financial institutions. Cryptocurrencies have become a worldwide phenomenon, and most people are aware of them. There is a rising need to define cryptocurrencies' basic concept and functioning since even scientists, bankers, consultants, and engineers have limited comprehension of them. They also have trouble grasping even the most basic concepts.

3.1 Cryptocurrency Mining

3.1.1 How does Mining Work?

Mining is the process of creating new bitcoins or cryptocurrencies. Let's have a look at how mining works:

When you transmit money from your wallet to another person's wallet, your transactions go into the "mempool." The Bitcoin mempool is a collection of all transactions that have yet to be confirmed by the network. Miners gather transactions in specified blocks and then attempt to place them into the Blockchain, governed by their criteria. Every 10 minutes, a new block is generated in the Blockchain. A miner is a node on the network that collects and organizes transactions into blocks. When a transaction is complete, all network nodes receive it and check its authenticity. Miner nodes then collect these transactions from the memory pool and organize them into a candidate block.

For mining a block, a miner receives a reward. The reward is now 12 bitcoins. You will receive such a reward if you add a well-formed block into the system. Satoshi Nakamoto, by the way, produced the first (Genesis) block. Anyone may locate it and sell it for 50 bitcoins. The prize for a perfectly built block is starting to fall today. It is predicted that by the year 2140, it will have dropped to a tiny amount. Miners eventually understood that mining alone was no longer lucrative. The chance of finding such a block is determined by the "hash rate" or the computing power of your Bitcoin miner. If your hash rate is 10% of the total hash rate, you will be able to locate such blocks with a 10% chance and receive your reward under specific conditions. So, if you just mine from home on your laptop, you'll never locate a new block. As a result, miners band together in so-called mining pools to receive a more consistent payout. They take use of their combined hash rate to gain more consistent revenues. Many miners are asking themselves, "Why should I mine when I can purchase Bitcoin?" That's also a fantastic concept because Bitcoin's worth is established only by the belief of individuals who use it, whereas its price is determined by demand. It will cost you nothing if no one buys your Bitcoin. As a result, the value of Bitcoin will rise as long as people regard this technology as a way to utilize it anonymously, make huge payments, and so on.

     Cryptocurrency Investing For Beginners

The first benefit is that transaction costs are low. However, we must remember that Bitcoin is insufficient for micropayments. You will not be charged a dime if you send someone $1 million. If you elect to pay for a cup of coffee, however, the costs will be substantial in comparison to the cost of the coffee. The second benefit is the ability to execute transactions quickly. There are a few snags as well. In reality, every 10 minutes, a new block is generated in the Blockchain, implying that the quickest transaction takes ten minutes. Compared to a bank SWIFT transfer, which might take 2 to 4 days, this appears to be rather speedy. Visa and MasterCard, on the other hand, are speedier. They can process tens of thousands of times the number of transactions per unit of time as Bitcoin. It's worth mentioning that various sorts of cryptocurrencies are currently created to be quicker than Bitcoin. The pseudo-anonymity of participants is the third advantage. We've previously established that anybody can monitor all network transactions. You can follow all transactions carried out from a wallet if you know who owns it. As a result, Bitcoin cannot be described as completely anonymous. Anonymity vanishes as soon as one can connect your address to your personality. However, if you practice "internet hygiene," which means you don't disclose your wallet to anybody, your transactions can't be monitored. However, alternative cryptocurrencies that are more anonymous than Bitcoin should be included. By the way, keeping your identity hidden while transacting on the Bitcoin network is already doable. There is a slew of firms that will clean your bitcoins. They're known as "mixing services," and they're used to mix one's bitcoins with other people's, obfuscating the trail back to the money's source.

As you can see, new technologies have emerged to improve cryptocurrency anonymity. Finally, more than 16 million bitcoins are currently in circulation worldwide, with a total of 21 million expected to be produced. The network's algorithm is responsible for programming such figures. Bitcoin's restricted supply prevents it from becoming inflationary. Because only a limited amount of this currency will be created, it will not devalue over time. Bitcoin has a deflationary approach: many users lose their coins because they forget their wallet password or send money to the wrong address. As a result, the number of bitcoins will steadily decline.

3.2 How are Transactions Confirmed?

A cryptocurrency such as Bitcoin consists of a peer network. Each peer has a record of all transactions' full history and, therefore, every account's balance. A transaction is a file that states, "Bob provides Alice with X Bitcoin" and is signed by a private key of Bob. It is simple cryptography with a public key, nothing special at all. After signing, a transaction is broadcast on the network, transmitted from one peer to every peer. This is a simple infrastructure for peer-to-peer.

3.3 Properties of Cryptocurrency

Bitcoin is a decentralized peer network that maintains accounts and balances consensus. It is more like a currency than the numbers in your bank account that you see. What are these numbers more than database entries, a database that can be altered by persons you don't see and by laws you don't know? Cryptocurrencies are essentially token entries in decentralized consensus databases. They are called cryptocurrencies as good cryptography secures the consensus-keeping method. Cryptocurrencies are built on cryptography. They are not covered by people or by trust but by mathematics. It is more likely that your house will collapse on an asteroid than that a Bitcoin address will be stolen. We ought to differentiate between monetary and transactional properties when defining the properties of cryptocurrencies.

3.3.1 Irreversible

After confirmation, nobody can reverse a transaction.

3.3.2 Pseudonymous

Neither accounts nor transactions are linked to names in the real world. On so-called addresses, you obtain Bitcoins. If the transaction flow can typically be studied, it is not generally possible to associate users' real-world identities with such addresses.

3.3.3 Fast and Global

Transactions are immediately exchanged on the network and are validated within a few minutes. The physical location is not affected because they exist in a global network of machines. If you give Bitcoin to your neighbor or someone from the other side of the globe, it doesn't matter.

3.3.4 Secure

In a public key cryptography system, cryptocurrency funds are stored. Cryptocurrency can be sent only by the private key owner. Strong cryptography and the magic of large numbers make this scheme impossible to break. More secure than Fort Knox is a Bitcoin address.

3.3.5 Does Not Require Any Permission

You don't have to request someone for a cryptocurrency to use. It's all apps that can be downloaded for free for anyone. You can receive and transfer Bitcoins or other cryptocurrencies after installing them. No one's trying to block you. No gatekeeper is here.

3.3.6 Controlled Supply

Most cryptocurrencies constrain the availability of tokens. In Bitcoin, supply declines in time, and sometime around the year 2140 will hit its final amount. All cryptocurrencies manage the distribution of the token through a schedule written in the code. This suggests that the money supply can be approximately estimated currently about any given time in the future.

3.3.7 No Debt Yet Bearer

The Fiat money is created by debt in your bank account, and the numbers you see on your ledger reflect nothing but debts. Cryptocurrencies are not debt; they are all self-represented. You must consider all properties to understand the groundbreaking effect of cryptocurrencies. Bitcoin is an assault on banks and governments' power over their people's money transactions as a permission-free, permanent, and pseudonymous payment medium. You can't block anyone from using Bitcoin, you can't ban someone from making a payment, and you can't cancel a transaction. Cryptocurrencies attack the scope of monetary policy as money with a restricted and regulated supply that is not modifiable by a state, a bank, or any other central entity. They strip away central banks' influence on inflation or deflation by controlling the money supply.

                        Cryptocurrency Investing For Beginners

3.4 Cryptocurrency — A Step Towards a New Economy

Cryptocurrencies are precious digital gold. It is sound cash, which is protected from political interference. Money promises, over time, to maintain and improve its worth. Cryptocurrencies on a global scale are also a kind of fast and convenient means of payment. They are private and confidential enough to assist black markets and some other outlawed commercial practices as a source of payment. Though cryptocurrencies are primarily used for payment, the payment components are dwarfed by their usage as a medium of gambling and the outlet of wealth. Cryptocurrencies gave rise to an increasingly competitive market for buyers and speculators that is rapidly increasing. Exchanges such as Poloniex, Okcoin, or Shapeshift allow hundreds of the cryptocurrencies to exchange. Their actual trading rate matches that of the main stock exchanges in Europe. Around a similar time, the (ICO) Initial Coin Distribution practice, often facilitated by the smart contracts of Ethereum, gives life to extremely successful crowd financing ventures, where an idea is always enough to raise millions of dollars. You are witnessing intense volatility in this rich world of coins & tokens.

3.5 Cryptocurrency List

Although Bitcoin remains the most popular cryptocurrency by far yet, most similar cryptocurrencies have negligible non-speculative effects, and other cryptocurrencies should be kept in mind by investors and consumers. The most common cryptocurrencies today are listed below:

3.5.1 Bitcoin

In the entire cryptocurrency business, Bitcoin, the initial and the most popular cryptocurrency, acts as the digital standard of gold. It is utilized as a worldwide payment mechanism like darknet markets or ransomware's de-facto money of the cybercrime.

3.5.2 Ethereum

In the hierarchy of cryptocurrencies, talented crypto-genius Vitalik Buterin has risen to a secondary place. In comparison to Bitcoin, the blockchain validates a series of accounts & balances and so-called different states. This suggests that Etherium can process transfers and intricate contracts and systems. This versatility makes Ethereum the right method for implementing the blockchain. It arrives at a premium, though. The developers agreed to create a hard fork without agreement after the DAO hack, an Ethereum-consisted smart contract, culminating in the Ethereum Classic appearance. In addition, there are numerous Ethereum copies, and Ethereum is itself the host of the several DigixDAO & Augur tokens. This makes Ethereum a collection rather than the single currency of cryptocurrencies.

3.5.3 Ripple

Although Ripple has an indigenous cryptocurrency, XRP, IOUs processing is more regarding the network than the cryptocurrency itself. The currency does not exist to store & exchange the value as a medium but rather as a token to secure the network from spam. Unlike Bitcoin & Ethereum, Ripple has no mining because all the coins are already pre-mined. As a number of the banks have entered the network of Ripple, Ripple has seen tremendous importance in the financial room.

3.5.4 Litecoin

After Bitcoin, Litecoin was among the first crypto coins, and the digital Bitcoin gold was branded as silver. With a bigger token & a revolutionary mining algorithm, the Litecoin was the true breakthrough quicker than Bitcoin, better suited to be Bitcoin's smaller sibling. It encouraged the advent of many other cryptocurrencies that used codebase but created it lighter, even more so. Feathercoin or Dogecoin are examples. Although after Bitcoin, Litecoin struggled to find the real usage case & lost its secondary spot, it still is extensively pursued & traded; then if Bitcoin fails, it is usually hoarded as the replacement.

3.5.5 Monero

The most famous instance of the Crypto Night algorithm is Monero. Any transaction is recorded inside the blockchain if you are a Bitcoin user, and the trace of transactions could be traced. The Crypto Night algorithm was capable to break through the trail with the implementation of the concept called the ring signatures. Byte coin, the first Crypto Night implementation, was heavily pre-mined, and thus it is refused by the crowd. Monero was Byte Coin's first non-pre-mined clone & raised ample popularity. Many other crypto note incarnations with their little enhancements, but none of them have ever gained the same success as Monero. In the summer of 2016, after several darknet markets agreed to embrace it as the currency, Monero's success peaked. This culminated in a gradual price rise, though Monero's real use remains poor, disappointingly. There are, besides those, hundreds of multi-family cryptocurrencies. Some of them are just nothing more than efforts to reach customers and make money fast, but all offer playgrounds to examine cryptocurrency technologies.

3.6 The Evolution of the Cryptocurrencies

Over time, a standard type of cryptocurrency has greatly grown. Stable coins and cryptocurrencies, which use a special type of cryptography to stay stable in price, are among the most important crypto implementations. There are 3 types of stable coins inside the market:

- Crypto-backed

- Fiat-backed

- Algorithm-based

Given below are the reasons behind the popularity of stable cryptocurrency coins.

3.6.1 The Best of All Worlds

The reality that gives you the best of all worlds, i.e., fiat & crypto, is one of the most enticing characteristics of safe coins. Generally, lack of stability & extreme uncertainty is

                                   Cryptocurrency Investing For Beginners

referred to as the key factors holding back the acceptance of cryptography. Stable coins, however, totally alleviate this dilemma by maintaining price consistency. However, regardless of this, it is all centered on blockchain technology, which offers you the advantages of blockchain technology found in immutability and decentralization.

3.6.2 DApps

As the finance's future and among the greatest boosters of the adoption of blockchain, Decentralized Finance (DeFi) is already touted. With ease, you can usually combine numerous DeFi applications/products. To facilitate in-app transactions and create an internal economy, stable coins can be conveniently incorporated with DeFi applications.

3.6.3 Faster Remittance

Stable coins enable you to make transfers and remittances cross-border at a significantly rapid rate.

3.7 Blockchain and Cryptocurrency

The transaction is nearly instantly broadcast to the whole network, but it is only confirmed when time has passed. Validation is a significant phrase in the world of cryptocurrency. You might say that cryptocurrencies are all about validation and verification. As long as a transaction is unconfirmed, it is pending and can be falsified. Until a contract is verified, it is fixed in stone. It can't be fabricated, and it can't be reversed. The so-called blockchain is a sort of immutable record of previous transactions. Miners are the only ones who can verify transactions. This is their function in a cryptocurrency network. They take lawful purchases and spread them around the network. After the miner validates the transaction, every node must add this to its database. The blockchain has had a role in this. Miners are rewarded with a cryptocurrency token for their efforts, such as Bitcoins.

3.8 What is Blockchain, and How does it Work?

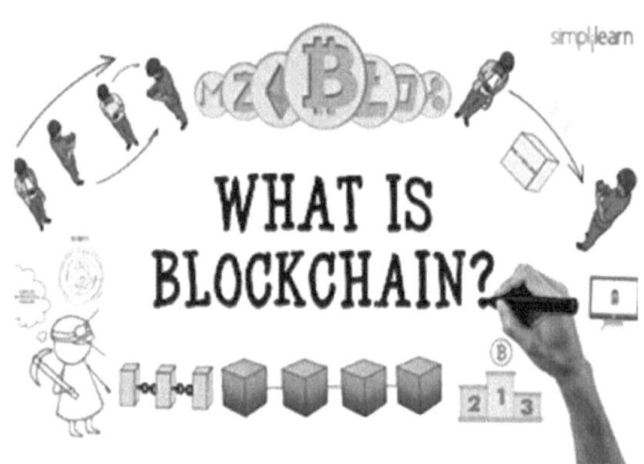

Before delving into the technical aspects of Blockchain technology, it's critical to grasp the challenges that Blockchain addresses. What makes Blockchain so important, and what can it achieve that our existing technology can't? Early users of Bitcoin and Blockchain technology saw a fault in the way we think about transactions, trust, and social institutions that they saw as fundamental. The first versions of Blockchain appeared around the United States' financial crisis in 2007 when many individuals lost trust in social institutions that were intended to defend the common person's interests. People were disillusioned with the banking system after the crisis and the government's ability to oversee financial markets, and the press' ability to probe prospective problems. Our institutions, most people would agree, have problems and aren't ideal answers. They do, however, fix trust issues, and they've done so for hundreds of years. Indeed, we are most likely living in the calmest and most pleasant period in human history. Any alternative to our present institutions must have a clear set of benefits and advantages. Blockchain aims to replace institutions controlled by flawed humans with technology that can perform a better job while simultaneously empowering individuals. You'd solve one of society's largest bottlenecks if you could make it possible for strangers to trust one another without needing a bank or government to act as a middleman. But you'd need a powerful method for reaching consensus among strangers, and Blockchain's architects think that power resides in decentralization. The principle of decentralization is at the heart of all Blockchain (and other cryptographic technology) applications. Blockchain aims to return regulatory power to individuals rather than a strict, sluggish central authority making choices and controlling interactions. Rather than relying on a large organization, Blockchain establishes confidence through consensus.

Blockchain combines encryption and a public ledger to establish trust between participants in its most basic form while preserving anonymity. Understanding the mechanics of how this works is a little more complex, but we'll need to go into the technical specifics to grasp Blockchain technology's genius properly. While Blockchain can have many more characteristics, the technology's name encapsulates the fundamentals: A block is a collection of transactions from a specific period. It holds all of the data that has been processed on the network in the last several minutes. Only one block is created at a time by the network. The chain: utilizing cryptographic techniques, each block is connected to the one before it. These algorithms are complex for computers to calculate, and even the world's fastest computers can take several minutes to solve them. The cryptographic chain locks the block into place after it is solved, making it difficult to modify. In a moment, we'll take a closer look at this. Over time, the chain lengthens. Once a new block is formed, the computers on the network collaborate to validate the block's transactions and protect its position in the chain. The ledger is the most basic component of the Blockchain. It's where you'll get information on the accounts on the network. The Blockchain's ledger takes the place of a bank or other institution's ledger. This ledger typically contains account numbers, transactions, and balances for a cryptocurrency. When you submit a transaction to the Blockchain, you're updating the ledger with information on where the currency is coming from and going to. A Blockchain ledger is a distributed ledger that is shared across the network. Every node in the network maintains its copy of the ledger, updated whenever a new transaction is submitted. Blockchain aims to replace banks and other organizations through this "shared ledger." Rather than having the bank store a single official copy of the ledger, everyone will keep their copy, and we will then validate transactions by consensus. Each Blockchain system has its ledger, which works in various ways (as we'll see). To post a transaction on the Bitcoin ledger, the first Blockchain ledger, three pieces of information are required:

 Cryptocurrency Investing For Beginners

1. **An input:** If John wishes to transfer David a Bitcoin, he must first inform the network of how he obtained the Bitcoin. The first section of the ledger record indicates that John got the Bitcoin from Sarah yesterday.

2. **Amount:** This is the money John wishes to transfer to David.

3. **An output:** David's Bitcoin address and the location where the Bitcoin should be placed.

The next tough notion of understanding is that there is no such thing as a Bitcoin. There are no tangible Bitcoins, of course. That's probably something you already knew. However, there are no Bitcoins stored on a hard disc. "This is a Bitcoin," you can't say that pointing to a real thing, a digital file, or a piece of code. Instead, the Bitcoin network is nothing more than a collection of transaction records. The Bitcoin Blockchain's distributed ledger contains every transaction in Bitcoin's history. If you want to verify that you have 20 Bitcoins, you can only do so by referring to the transactions where those 20 Bitcoins were received. This is a feature that almost all Blockchains share. The currency is the history of transactions. There isn't any distinction between the two. Some new cryptocurrencies are changing how the ledger is written to increase transaction anonymity and privacy. They conceal the source and recipient of the transaction while maintaining a functionally distributed ledger by employing identity masking techniques.

3.8.1 Creating a Block

The ledger is the heart of the block, but it isn't the only thing that goes into a new one. For each block, a header and a footer are necessary. Additionally, the transactions in the block go through compression, encoding, and standardization procedure. When a validator constructs a new block, it looks nothing like the ledger on which it was based. On the other hand, the underlying ledger remains intact and may be accessed in the future if new transactions require information from prior blocks.

3.8.2 Adding Transactions

Gathering and uploading all current transactions to the block's ledger is the initial stage in constructing a block. When a user initiates a new transaction, the transaction is broadcast to the whole network. A verifier's computer will next review the transaction to ensure it is genuine. Because Blockchain currencies are nothing more than a series of transactions, the first step in verifying a transaction is to look at the sender's stated source of funds. The verifier will next search the Blockchain's history for the block and transaction where the sender received the money. If the input transaction is verified on the Blockchain, the transaction is legitimate, and the receiving party's address must be validated. If the input transaction hasn't been confirmed, the current transaction is invalid, and it won't be added to the ledger. It's time to build the ledger when all of the transactions in that block have been validated. Here's a simple example in which the transactions are listed sequentially:

[Input][Amount][Output address], [Input][Amount]
[Output address], [Input] [Amount][Output address], [Input
[Amount][Output address], [Input][Amount] [Output address]...

The verifier will next perform hashing (a cryptographic method) on each transaction. Hashing takes a string of characters and creates another string of characters in its most basic form. So, if you provide a hashing algorithm for the input, amount, and output address, it will transform the transaction into a string of characters that is unique to that transaction, like this:

aba128d3931e54ce63a69d8c2c1c705ea9f39ca950df13655d92db662515eacf

(This is a Bitcoin transaction hash taken from the blockchain)

As a result, hashing is utilized to standardize data while ensuring it is not tampered with. If someone tried to modify a transaction on the Blockchain, they'd have to rehash it, which would result in a whole different transaction, and the reality that it had been tampered with would be clear. Most blockchains often hash to make it even more difficult to tamper with the blockchain and to lower the amount of memory required to keep the transaction ledger. This means they mix the hash of one transaction with the hash and re-hash the result into a new smaller hash. A Merkle Tree is created by combining transactions in this fashion, and the root hash of all transactions is provided at the start of the block. Understanding why we need a Merkle Tree is the subject of a more in-depth book, but the Merkle Tree, at its most basic level, ensures that all transactions in a block are legitimate while consuming less memory in the long term.

3.8.3 Time Stamp and the Block ID

The time stamp and any block ID information are the final elements of a block, making it simple to go back and check prior blocks afterward. Future transactions will be able to reference this block ID as the block holding the current transaction's input transaction (also known as the "coinbase").

3.8.4 Linking Blocks Together

The last stage of making a block is connecting it to the preceding blocks in the chain. There are various ways to achieve this, but almost all of them use some form of hashing to make the previous block's content part of the current block. Keep in mind that hashing converts any input into a string of letters, no matter how large or tiny. If you adjust the input even a little, it affects the entire output. We may take the hash of the entire previous block and append it to the beginning of the following block to include the contents of the previous block in the current block. By doing so, we've essentially connected the old and new blocks because any change in the older block, no matter how minor, will affect the hash of the entire block. It is now far more challenging to modify a block once it has been built. You'd have to re-hash the whole block if you made an update to an older block. After re-hashing block 1, you'll need to crack open block 2, remove block 1's old hash, input block 1's new hash, and then re-hash block 2. However, because new blocks are generated, changing a previous transaction would need editing every block made after that transaction.

The longer it takes to hack the network and successfully modify a transaction, the more difficult it gets. Hashing is at the heart of Blockchain security for this reason. The encryption makes it impossible to alter the transaction ledger, allowing it to be public and secure. The hashing, on the other hand, is not complex. In a matter of seconds, most computers could rehash a Blockchain. So, to ensure that the hashing security performs its job, we must make the production of a new block more difficult. Ideally, it should be something that slows down an attacker and increases the chances of honest network members winning. The increased difficulty is known as "proof of work" in the Bitcoin Blockchain (and most other current blockchains).

3.8.4 Hash Rate

https://blockchain.info/charts/hash-rate displays the current hash rate. It shows that the pace has been gradually increasing over time and that it is now at 31 million terahashes per second (TH/s). Because 1 terahash already equals 10, 12 1,000,000,000,000, or one trillion hashes, this is an exceptionally large quantity. Can you imagine how much computer power is required to compute 1 trillion hashes each second? Imagine that number is increased by 30 million. That is the degree of hashing that is now taking place in the Bitcoin mining sector to keep the currency alive. Every second, all of the world's miners calculate 31,000,000,000,000,000,000 — thirty-one million trillion hashes. The greater the number of miners online, the higher the difficulty will rise. Miners compete to be the first to solve the riddle and earn the reward, which is now 12.5 Bitcoins. Every 10 minutes, 12.5 Bitcoins are distributed throughout the day. That means 75 Bitcoins are up for grabs every hour. At today's market value of approximately 10,000 dollars, mining may earn you $750,000 every day. This is why so many miners are flooding the market since there is a lot of money to be made. However, the system is designed to make the challenge more complex as hash power increases. The Bitcoin creators intended for a regular period between new Bitcoins to be released into the population. Remember that Bitcoin is only distributed as a reward for miners' contributions to mining. The system checks the online hash rate and the time it took to answer the past five problems to maintain this around 10 minutes (or near to it).

3.9 Blockchain: Opinion or Science?

Blockchain technology is no more an idea and has become the latest technological invention of the 21st century. Its origin and popularity are backed by the endorsement of scientific processes, as illustrated below:

From its beginnings as pure digital money in 2008/2009, the distributed ledger technology (DLT) blockchain has grown to encompass various uses. The term "blockchain" refers to the grouping of bitcoin transactions into data blocks that include a unique, complicated trace ("hash"/"Merkle tree") of their predecessors. One particular block is chosen, time-stamped, and updated to an immutable and unforgeable distributed ledger file, which is replicated on numerous separate nodes using a well-defined consensus mechanism. In the absence of intermediaries, decentralized computing, storage, and transaction fees ensure trust inside this peer-to-peer network. The complex interplay of these procedures guards against malicious spamming, fraudulent identity generation, and hostile takeover attempts. Crypto-economic incentives promote contributions from the "crowd" to keep the blockchain operational. Cryptoassets can be exchanged into fiat money on secondary exchanges, used to pay utility bills, staked for credibility, or granted voting rights under a liquid-democracy-style government. Transactions can be linked to a code safely stored on the decentralized ledger and run on its decentralized virtual machine ("EVM"), which was first enabled on the Ethereum blockchain. These "smart contracts" can accept information from reliable on-chain or appropriately staked off-chain sources to trigger conditionals. Such as programmable money expands into the ("DApps") decentralized applications that have already demonstrated many compelling cases of use, such as decentralized finance, supply chain management, asset, and provenance tracking, e.g., for physical and digital collectibles or food, wrapped in convenient browser interfaces. Non-fungible tokens (NFTs), which represent a digital certificate of (potentially partial) ownership reflecting a unique real-world item such as property, commodities, or artwork, are another noteworthy crypto-economically enabled the feature of blockchain. Without intermediaries, blockchain can establish a self-sovereign identity to appropriately attribute credentials in research and education. While blockchain technology has its roots in cryptography, finance, and computer science, it has advanced at a fast pace over the last decade as a result of often-unprecedented collaborations with a diverse range of fields, including economics, game theory, banking, risk management, data science, data security, identity management, logistics, supply chains, trading, education, law, administration, governance, political science, psychology, ethics, arts, and social sciences. Blockchain technology's extraordinary interdisciplinarity has proven to be a significant source of innovation. This viewpoint simply identifies notable parallels between scientific discovery and blockchain processes. In many ways, the token economy powered by blockchain ("tokenization") holds enormous promise for increasing critical community participation to increase the quality, credibility, adoption, and impact of research outputs. New IP and data can be time-stamped and unquestionably lodged as NFTs on the blockchain as proof of knowledge for securely asserting (co-)authorship, inventorship, and ownership, with blockchain-based (self-sovereign) identity management.

CHAPTER 4

How to Invest in Cryptocurrency

We invest in something if we consider it worthwhile. We will first describe some of the important advantages and disadvantages of investing in cryptocurrency to help you make the right decision.

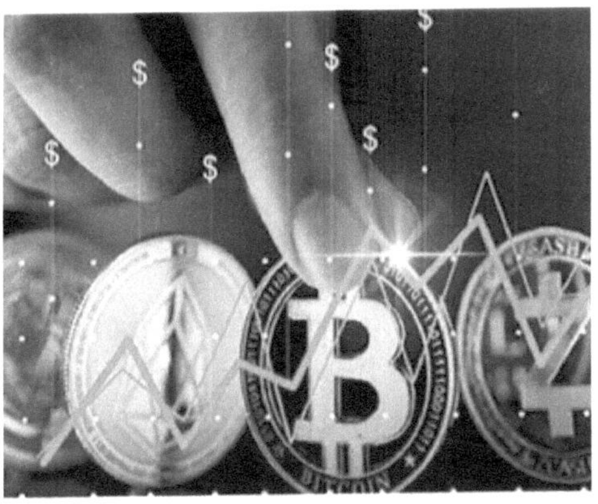

4.1 Advantages of Investing in Cryptocurrency

Listed below are the prime benefits of investing in cryptocurrency:

4.1.1 Greater Liquidity

Cryptocurrency like bitcoin has much greater liquidity than its rivals, becoming the most common cryptocurrency by a large distance. This helps consumers transition to fiat currencies, including the U.S. dollar and the euro, to maintain much of their underlying value. On the other side, many other cryptocurrencies will not be explicitly substituted for fiat currencies or risk losing considerable value throughout certain transactions.

4.1.2 Wide Acceptance as a Payment Method

Hundreds approve payments of bitcoin cryptocurrency of retailers. It is possible to purchase almost any physical object using Bitcoin units due to heavyweights like Overstock.com hopping on board. Bitcoin's rising mass adoption is likely to be a huge aid if you're concerned about decreasing your exposure to fiat currencies.

4.1.3 International Transactions Easier than with Regular Currencies

There is little difference between Bitcoin transactions crossing foreign boundaries and Bitcoin transactions that remain in the country. As is always the case for credit card charges, ATM cash deposits, and overseas money transfers, there are no international processing costs or red tape to follow. Although international red tape is absent in most other cryptocurrencies, cross-border Bitcoin transfers are smoother precisely because Bitcoin is more common worldwide.

 Cryptocurrency Investing For Beginners

4.1.4 Lower Transaction Fee

Bitcoin comes with lesser processing costs than other digital payment types, like credit cards and PayPal. Although such payments are unpredictable, costing more than 1% of their value is uncommon for a Bitcoin transaction.

4.1.5 Offer Anonymity and Privacy as Compared to Traditional Currencies

The built-in privacy provisions of Bitcoin allow users if they wish, to fully isolate their Bitcoin accounts from the public personas. Although monitoring Bitcoin flows between users is possible, it's very hard to determine who those users are.

4.1.6 Free From Political Agents and Creators

Because any state body, such as a central bank, does not create or regulate Bitcoin, it is not subject to political interference. It is also much tougher for regimes to freeze or capture Bitcoin units, either in legal criminal proceedings or as a penalty for political activities, as is often the case in authoritarian states such as Russia and China, since it operates outside any political framework.

4.1.7 Built-in Scarcity

The built-in scarcity attribute of Bitcoin is expected to help its long-term value against conventional currencies and non-scarce cryptocurrencies. Only 21 million may remain (such as Dogecoin, a popular Bitcoin alternative). Bitcoin's rarity imbues the currency with inherent worth close to gold and other precious metals.

4.1.8 Personal Information Privacy

If you wish to buy something from a store and pay with a credit card, you should hand over your credit card to the store. To make a payment, you must show the seller your pin code. Which method do you think is the safest? Your pin code is very private, and you do not need to divulge it. With cryptocurrencies, this isn't an issue. You are not required to share your private key with anyone. Even your money will be encrypted; no one will be able to see your payment information, and it will never be leaked. As a result, it's the best option for making anonymous payments.

4.1.9 Instant and Secure Transfer

You have a precious asset on your hands if you have cryptocurrency in your digital wallet. It's simple to give it to anyone without soliciting their permission. You'll need the other person's private key to complete the transfer. There is no cost to transferring ownership, no uncomfortable situations will arise, and no paperwork will be required. In contrast to other instances like property transfer or bank account closure, you must complete substantial documentation and pay a commission.

4.1.10 Anti-Inflation Characteristics

The value of numerous currencies has dropped over time due to inflation. Almost every cryptocurrency was released with a predetermined supply when it first came out. Every currency's number is stated in its source code; for instance, around 21 million Bitcoins are in circulation worldwide. As a result, with an increase in demand, its value also increases. This prevents you from the impact of inflationary pressure in the long term.

 Cryptocurrency Investing For Beginners

4.1.11 No Mediatory

Bitcoin has several advantages, one of which is generally decentralized. Most of the cryptocurrencies are usually controlled by the developers who use them and all those who own a large quantity of the money or by the company that creates it before it is released. In contrast to fiat currencies, which the government controls, decentralization keeps the currency free of monopoly and in check by ensuring that no single institution controls the movement and value of the coins. This, in turn, makes it stable & safe.

4.1.12 Self-Managed and Regulated

Any currency's governance and maintenance are crucial to its growth. Developers and miners store bitcoin transactions on their hardware and are compensated with a transaction fee. Miners are compensated for their efforts, keeping transaction records accurate and up to date, safeguarding the integrity of the coins, and keeping data decentralized.

4.2 Disadvantages of Investing in Cryptocurrency

Listed below are the disadvantages of investing in cryptocurrency:

4.2.1 Money Disruption

A controversy over the underlying existence of money and the sustainability of conventional banking and financial markets has been sparked by the exponential growth of cryptocurrencies. Although speculators have flocked with extreme enthusiasm to virtual currency, skilled investors have generally adopted a more conservative approach.

4.2.2 Vulnerability to Scams

Cryptocurrencies seem to have more than their fair share of medium-specific scams, theft, and threats. These vary from minor Ponzi schemes, like Bitcoin Savings & Trust, to major hacking attacks, such as Sheep Marketplace and Mt. Gox infringements.

4.2.3 Black Market Activity Damages Reputation of Cryptocurrency

To hackers and grey market players, cryptocurrency remains appealing. Dark network markets such as Silk Road and Sheep expose rank-and-file consumers to theft and the possibility of criminal prosecution. More troublingly, Bitcoin's reputation is undermined by advancing nefarious activity by supposedly upstanding Bitcoin users, such as Charlie Shrem.

4.2.4 High Price Volatility

While the most stable and readily traded cryptocurrency is Bitcoin, it remains vulnerable to severe price fluctuations over brief periods. Bitcoin's worth dropped by more than 50% after the Mt. Gox crash. Moreover, Bitcoin's value spiked by an almost identical amount soon after the FBI's declaration; it will treat Bitcoin and other virtual currencies as legitimate financial services. Bitcoin's valuation doubled several times in late 2017, only to halve in the first weeks of 2018, wiping out billions nearly overnight in market value. While the instability of Bitcoin often provides risky traders with short-term gains, it makes the asset unsuitable for longer time horizons for more cautious investors.

4.2.5 No Refunds

One of the main disadvantages of cryptocurrency is the absence of a standardized chargeback or refund scheme, as both credit card providers and conventional online payment processing providers. Via cryptocurrency, consumers impacted by purchase theft cannot seek a refund. The decentralized nature of cryptocurrency renders it difficult for any entity to arbitrate conflicts amongst users. Though miners take responsibility for transaction documentation, they cannot judge their legality.

4.2.6 Chance of Performing Illegal Activity

Because bitcoin transactions have such a high level of confidentiality and anonymity, it is difficult for authorities to track down or maintain track of any user based on their wallet address. On the other hand, Bitcoin has been utilized to carry out various illegal activities in the past, including the purchase of narcotics on the darker web. Furthermore, some people use bitcoin to conceal the origins of their unlawfully obtained money by converting it through a trusted intermediary.

4.2.7 High Loss Risk

The lack of ownership and control over cryptocurrency is a self-risk. If something goes wrong, you have no recourse. You can't protect your bitcoin from being lost due to a wallet malfunction. You cannot make a claim since this money is not under the control of any company. If you are having difficulty, you are unable to tell anyone about it. So, if you choose a wallet, be sure it has positive reviews and can be trusted. Another thing to consider before using cryptocurrencies is that you are familiar with the current cryptocurrency rules in your country.

4.3 The Basic Fundamentals of Investing

New challenges and frequently changing conditions or scenarios help you to train and prepare for complex situations. Prices in Capital and Currency Markets of the world do not depict a stereotype or lackluster behavior. Prices do not move in a straight line and are susceptible to frequent changes. These price changes transpire even in the short time span of a second. Price changes give a wavy appearance to prices when these are plotted on the graph. All investment decisions aim to generate money smartly and efficiently while keeping the risk factors to the minimum. As a prudent investor, you have to decide to select the best investment opportunity from the available options. You, being the investor, will be guided in your quest by researching for answers to different critical questions, such as:

- What investment option offers the most secure return concerning investment time?

Cryptocurrency Investing For Beginners

- Where is that particular investment option currently in its business cycle?

- When is the best time for committing the investment amount?

Prices, as mentioned above, do not move in a straight line, and the price activity is shaped by scores of factors stemming from changes in political and industrial policies to frequent shifts in international business supply and demand factors. This standard operating procedure is also followed in the Capital and Currency Markets with the addition of another crucial factor that attempts to seek and investigate the reasons behind such an investment decision. Succinctly, an investment decision on cryptocurrency revolves around the three W's.

1. What to buy or trade

2. Why buy or trade

3. When to buy or trade

An investment or trading decision, no matter how smart, could result in the wiping of funds if not exquisitely timed. Besides, you also have to address and define the risk factor and profit objective. All investments are made in pursuit of profit. The profit objective has to be ascertained at the time of investment or trading decision to help you exit successfully from the market.

4.3.1 Have Knowledge of Risks Associated with Cryptocurrency

Given below is a brief overview of risks associated with cryptocurrencies:

- **Market risks:** The threats involved with the trade-in cryptocurrencies are largely linked to their instability. They are volatile; abrupt fluctuations in market sentiment will lead to price swings that are sharp and sudden. The value of cryptocurrencies is not unusual to drop exponentially by hundreds, if not thousands of dollars.

- **Liquidity risks:** The currency is small, which means it can suffer from liquidity problems, and limited ownership can make it vulnerable to market manipulation. In addition, the currency can look more unpredictable than most other physical currencies, driven by speculative demand and aggravated by hoarding, provided its restricted adoption and lack of alternatives.

- **Exchange risks:** They can arise because of dispersed risk, anonymity, lack of control, and potential for significant loss.

- **Wallet risks:** Bitcoin wallets have a genuine weakness when it comes to malware attacks and stealing. A study by a team of Edinburgh University researchers said they find weak points that can be abused in hardware wallets. According to the same report, even the highly encrypted hardware wallets were still insecure because of the loophole.

- The researchers were able to intercept contact between the wallet and PCs using malware. This security violation compromises Bitcoin users' anonymity because their funds can be quickly diverted to other accounts.

- **Regulatory risks:** Efficient regulation of the cryptocurrency market would pass sophistication and stability to all legal virtual currencies, drawing institutional and private investors who will continue to treat them as a viable long-term investment rather than a short-term trading opportunity.

- **Scams:** Following factors can lead to scams, such as imposter websites, fake mobile apps, bad tweets, and scam emails.

4.4 Ways of Investing Inside the Cryptocurrency

While investing straight in cryptocurrencies is the most common method, traders also have other options, some of which are more direct than others. These are some of them:

4.4.1 Crypto Futures

The futures are another option to bet on Bitcoin price movements, and futures allow you to leverage your cash to produce the big profits (or the losses). Futures are the fast-paced market that magnifies crypto's already erratic movements.

4.4.2 Crypto Funds

There are also some crypto funds (like the Grayscale Trust of Bitcoin) that allow you to bet on the cost fluctuations of Bitcoin, Ethereum, and some other cryptocurrencies. As a result, they could be a convenient way to purchase cryptocurrency via the fund-type product.

4.4.3 Crypto Broker or Exchange Stocks

Investing inside the company that will profit from the emergence regardless of the cryptocurrency that wins could also be a good idea. And that's the possibility of an exchange like Coinbase or a broker like Robinhood, which relies heavily on crypto trading for revenue.

4.4.4 Blockchain ETFs

A blockchain exchange-traded fund (ETF) allows you to invest inside firms that may benefit from the rise of blockchain technology. The best blockchain ETFs provide you the exposure to a few of the most important publicly traded blockchain startups. However, it's worth noting that all these companies generally conduct a lot more than cryptocurrency-related activity, diluting your cryptocurrency exposure and lowering your potential gain and loss. Each of these options has a different level of risk and cryptocurrency exposure, so make sure you know exactly what you're getting and whether it meets your needs.

4.5 Short-Term

Let us be clear: short-term trading is not something we support. It has to do with one's personality. Short-term trading escapades, often known as speculative trading, excite some traders. Speculations make us sweat. We like to invest for the long term, sit back and relax, get a good night's sleep, and let the markets take care of themselves. Having said that, a lot of students come to me seeking short-term ideas. And, since we're such great instructors, we deliver. In this chapter, we'll go through some of the approaches we use to construct short-term plans that have worked for my students in the past. Although the fundamentals of short-term trading are similar across assets, crypto trading necessitates taking a few extra measures to improve your odds.

Aggressive trading is another phrase for short-term trading. Why? Because you're willing to take greater chances to generate more money. You must take greater risks to achieve a higher return. When attempting to gain money in the short term, you must also be willing to lose your investment (and maybe more!) in that time frame, particularly in a volatile market like cryptocurrency. Short-term trading may be classified into many categories based on how rapidly gains are realized—hours, days, or weeks. In general, the shorter the trading time frame, the greater the risk associated with that deal. The three most typical short-term trading time periods for cryptocurrencies are described in the sections below. This is what a day trader does if you've ever wondered what they do.

One type of aggressive short-term trading is day trading. You want to purchase and sell cryptos in a single day and profit before going to bed. A trading day in conventional markets, such as the stock market, typically finishes around

4:30 p.m. local time. However, because the bitcoin market is open 24 hours a day, you may tailor your day-trading hours to meet your schedule. Isn't it amazing? However, with tremendous power comes great responsibility. You don't want to lose your shirt and irritate your partner. Here are some things to ask yourself to see if day trading is the appropriate cryptocurrency path for you:

- Do you have the time to trade daily? Day trading is generally not for you if you have full-time work and can't stay glued to your computer all day. Make sure you're not trading during business hours! You may not only get fired, but you may also be unable to devote the necessary time and energy to trading. It's double the hassle.

- Do you have a high enough risk tolerance to engage in day trading?

- Are you prepared to risk losing money day trading even if you have the financial means to do so?

- Do you have the stomach to watch your investment portfolio fluctuate daily?

If not, day trading might not be for you. If you've decided that day trading is the crypto option for you, the sections below will provide you with some pointers to consider before getting started.

Define Crypto Trading Sessions

Because cryptocurrencies are exchanged across borders, one method to define a trading day is to look at trading sessions in financial centers such as New York, Tokyo, the eurozone (a group of European nations whose official currency is the euro), and Australia. These sessions are depicted in the diagram below. This strategy mimics the foreign currency (forex) market's trading sessions.

Some sessions may provide better trading opportunities if the cryptocurrency you're planning to trade has higher volume or volatility in that time frame. For example, a cryptocurrency based in China, such as NEO, may see more trading volume during the Asian session.

Know that Day Trading Cryptos is different from Day Trading Other Assets

When day trading traditional financial assets like stocks or currencies, you can look for pre-established fundamental market-movers like an upcoming earnings report or a country's interest rate decision. For the most part, the bitcoin market lacks a well-developed risk-event calendar. As a result, undertaking fundamental analysis to design a day trading strategy for cryptos is far more difficult.

Set a Time Aside

Depending on your own schedule, you might want to set aside time during the day to work on your trades. In principle, being able to trade at all hours of the day and night is a fantastic concept. You may just open your trading app during a restless night and begin trading. However, if you start losing sleep over it, this flexibility might backfire. It's critical to stay attentive throughout day trading or even night trading because you'll need to establish tactics, recognize trading opportunities, and manage your risk numerous times during the trading session. Having a clear discipline pays well for a lot of people.

4.6 How to Set Up the Digital Wallet

Digital wallets, also known as e-wallets, include the apps such as Google Pay, Apple Pay, and Samsung Pay and may be utilized to make the payments directly from your own phone or your smartwatch, eliminating the need to dig through your purse, fiddle using your wallet, and then rush to get the card or cash out. It's also a secure way to create payments using your phone. You might be wondering the difference between the e-wallet and the mobile wallet. While both have comparable functionality, the e-wallet could be used on various devices, including laptops, desktops, and mobile devices. In contrast, the mobile wallet can only be used on a mobile device.

Given below is the step-by-step procedure for setting up the digital wallet:

1. You have to ensure that the system operating on the mobile device is supported by Tap & Pay (5.0 + or iOS 8.1 + Android Lollipop).

2. The next step involves downloading the app for mobile payment of your preference. The good news is that several phones already have a payment app installed, so you can easily skip this step.

3. You can select to use Samsung Pay, Google Pay, or Apple Pay.

4. Follow the app's instructions on how actually to upload the financial information. The next step is to select your Summit debit or credit card as the default payment option. Uploading of the information can be made faster and easier by taking out a snapshot of the card during the process.

5. Now you are ready to use an e-wallet for making payments. Irrespective of whether you are in-store or at any other outlet, it is as easy as opening your e-wallet app and holding it next to the payment terminal. The process is similarly easy and fast while you are doing online shopping.

4.7 How do the Digital Wallets Actually Work?

An E-wallet is a secure and safe money management application or online platform that lets you make in-store purchases, send or transfer money, and keep track of rewarded programs. Also, you can easily link your e-wallet to bank accounts or use the prepay option to pay out as you move. It's easier than you think to replace your physical wallet (which, let's face it, contains primarily loose change & the old receipts anyhow) with a digital wallet. All of your summit debit and credit cards could be easily stored in the digital wallet on your own phone, prepared for usage online or in stores where the icon of the pay wave is displayed. Mobile payments operate in the same way as traditional transactions. Then all you got to do now is tap on your phone to complete the process. Isn't it quite easy?

4.8 Benefits of Using the Digital Wallet

Following are the advantages of using the digital wallet:

4.8.1 Security

It's difficult to tell which technological tools are truly secure, and digital wallets are among the most secure solutions available. If your wallet is stolen, your cash and credit cards are then gone in an instant. On the other hand, payment apps use encryption software, which means your data is safe and more unlikely to be actually hacked. In truth, digital wallet payments employ a token that is only valid at that merchant for that type of transaction rather than your actual card number. That means your personal information and credit card data will not be stolen if the store or firm encounters a cyber-attack.

4.8.2 Convenience

Not all merchants accept the digital type of transactions, yet the big majority have no objection to accepting the digital type of transactions. Moreover, a number of merchants are planning to provide all those services in the future. When you pay through the e-wallet, you are capable to execute transactions in a much faster, easier, and more protective way.

                        Cryptocurrency Investing For Beginners

4.8.3 Efficiency

Bid farewell to completing laborious checkout in the fields while shopping online or rummaging through the purse in the drive-through for your misplaced debit card. Your transactions will be seamless and straightforward, thanks to the e-wallet.

4.8.4 It is Free

Creating the shift from physical cards to cash is completely free of cost. The majority of transactions made with the e-wallet are free of charge.

CHAPTER 5

How do Crypto, NFT, ETF, and Metaverse Differ?

Metaverse, NFTs, ETFs, and the Crypto tokens are different entities. However, every one of these serves a distinct purpose while at the same time sharing and contributing to the growth of others. We will first briefly explain the concepts of Crypto tokens, NFT, ETF and Metaverse. We'll discuss how the Metaverse, NFT, and crypto tokens interact with each other. We will also try to understand why celebrities are flocking into the NFT space, which is again related to cryptocurrencies and Metaverse.

5.1 Crypto Tokens

Unlike cryptocurrency coins, their tokens do not really have their blockchain. They utilize the bitcoin blockchains inside their work. Ethereum, for instance, is utilized by numerous tokens, including stable coins. Cryptocurrency is an internet-based trading medium that uses cryptographic operations to perform financial transactions. Cryptocurrencies utilize blockchain technology to achieve decentralization, immutability, and accountability. They can be sent between two parties by the use of private and public keys. These transfers may be completed at limited processing rates, enabling customers to evade the large fees charged by the financial industry. Bitcoin is the first digital currency developed to fulfill that purpose. Cryptocurrency mining is a tool used to fix a cryptographic puzzle to construct blocks. Miners are compensated with the cryptocurrency.

The demand for cryptocurrencies is wild and fast. Almost every day, new cryptocurrencies rise, previous ones die, initial adopters get wealthy, and investors lose their money. Few last the first few months, and most of them are discarded by speculators. As a system for business micropayments, transactions, and preferred tool of remittance to replace Western Union, cryptocurrencies will gain legitimacy two years from now. With regard to market transfers, we may see two ways: there would be financial institutions using it for no fee and an almost instantaneous opportunity to move out any capital around. There will indeed be those who will need it with the blockchain infrastructure. Blockchain technology gives excellent benefits through trustless auditing, smart contracts, a singular source of reality, and color coins.

The truth is that cryptocurrency is here to stay and transform the universe. This is now occurring. People across the globe purchase Bitcoin to protect themselves from the depreciation of their domestic currency. Mainly inside Asia, a flourishing Bitcoin remittance industry has actually emerged, and the use of Bitcoin in cybercrime darknets is booming. Increasingly, businesses are leveraging the potential of the smart type of contracts or Ethereum tokens; the first use of the real-world blockchain is emerging. The number of retailers accepting Bitcoin is steadily growing. You can also buy furniture, plane tickets, and online writing facilities with Bitcoin. Remember, though, that before you go out and exchange your dollars for Bitcoin, Bitcoin has a long way to go before it's a tangible currency at the same level as the US dollar, euro, or pound. And there is no certainty that Bitcoin or any other non-national bank-regulated digital virtual currency would ever be a feasible substitute for traditional currencies, given that cryptocurrencies are enticing as a means of exchange. Some observers say that national governments will reorganize their currencies in the coming decades with state-sanctioned means of exchange that have certain cryptocurrency features, such as built-in scarcity and almost impenetrable counterfeit protection. Others believe that crypto and fiat cash will tend to coexist. Cryptocurrencies, however, would not expand beyond the current position of gold and other precious metals.

5.2 Metaverse

The metaverse is a 3D online universe made up of numerous virtual spaces. It's like a futuristic version of the internet. Users will be able to cooperate, meet, play games, and socialize in these 3D spaces with the metaverse. People will access the Metaverse using the Internet. In the Metaverse, technologies such as virtual reality (VR) as well as augmented reality (AR) are integrated to create a feel of virtual presence. Facebook defines Metaverse as a series of virtual environments where you can create and explore with other individuals who aren't in the same physical space as you. The Metaverse is also defined as an enormously scaled & the interoperable connection of real-time rendered virtual worlds of 3D that can be easily experienced persistently and synchronously by an effectively infinite amount of users who have a distinct feeling of presence, as well as data continuity like identity, history, communications, entitlements, objects, and payments.

Though the technology of Metaverse is still many years away from being fully realized, it is actually intended to be the virtual, online environment where you may work, play, learn, create, shop, as well as interact with others. The CEO of Facebook, Mark Zuckerberg, thinks that augmented reality (AR) glasses will soon become as popular as smartphones in the near future. The Metaverse is the type of a virtual world that mixes social networking, virtual reality (VR), online gaming, augmented reality (AR), and cryptocurrency to permit users to connect digitally. To improve users' experience, visual components, music, and other sensory input are superimposed on the real-world settings in augmented reality. On the other hand, virtual reality is entirely virtual and is used to enhance the imaginary worlds. As the Metaverse grows, it will create the online places that allow for more multidimensional interactions of the user than the current technology allows.

Users of the Metaverse will be able to participate in an environment where there is a mix of the physical and digital worlds, despite only viewing digital content.

5.3 NFT

NFT is an abbreviation for non-fungible tokens. NFTs are digital assets that may be purchased and traded via blockchain technology. They, as already mentioned, are not fungible, and are thus classified as a different form of asset, one based on value and popularity.

5.4 ETF

An ETF is a collection of securities whose shares are traded on a stock market. They blend the characteristics and potential benefits of stocks, mutual funds, and bonds. ETF shares, like individual stocks, are traded throughout the day at varying prices based on supply and demand. Like mutual fund shares, ETF shares represent a portion of ownership in a professionally managed portfolio. One of Metaverse's key goals is to make remote working feel less remote and provide users with a more intimate experience that resembles being in a room. Global assets are now streaming into new exchange-traded funds that offer exposure to companies competing to create virtual realities, signaling that the metaverse has fully entered the mainstream. However, because we are still in the early stages of this revolution, investors should consider investing in companies related to the Metaverse to earn attractive returns while stocks are still inexpensive. According to Bloomberg, ETF assets that focused on the metaverse have risen to $2.2 billion, thanks in part to Facebook's parent company changing its name from Facebook Inc. to Meta Platforms Inc. in October, indicating the growing importance of these new virtual communities.

The majority of new exchange-traded products have recently been introduced, and they're swiftly establishing themselves as a thriving market for thematic investment. According to a Bloomberg study, the Round Hill Ball Metaverse ETF (METV) is the industry leader, with $856 million under management. METV, in a crowded market, slashed management fees from 75 to 59 basis points this month, making it the cheapest fund in the category. The Subversive Metaverse ETF (PUNK) focuses on both domestic and international enterprises and has a 75 basis point expense ratio. Experience, discovery, creator economy, spatial computing, decentralization, human interface, and infrastructure are among the seven levels of the metaverse that the actively managed fund seeks out.

5.5 How do Crypto, NFT, and Metaverse Supplement Differ from Each Other?

The Metaverse is a virtual reality simulation. In these virtual worlds, users can use a virtual self (a made-to-order avatar that can look the way they choose) to attend events, visit art galleries, & travel to exotic locations. There are also several Metaverses. Other companies are also working on these with their own series of interconnected protocols. Every one of these Metaverses are working toward the same goal: better integrating our physical and digital lives. Cryptocurrencies are a type of digital asset used as a medium of exchange and a store of value in these virtual worlds. There, cryptos are digital assets used as a medium of exchange and a store of value. In contrast, cryptocurrencies are digital assets that are mostly used as the medium of exchange and a store of value in the real world. Indeed, NFTs allow one-of-a-kind digital artworks to be purchased or sold on the blockchain. Only some people can say to own a Monet when it comes to art. Others can make copies of the original, but they're not valued as much as the official version because the property isn't transferred like with an impression.

NFTs work on the same principle. The ownership of the NFT is verified on the blockchain via several network processes, ensuring that the authentic owner of any work of art is identified. While it may appear that everything is random, there is a connection between these blockchain occurrences. The technology of the black chain underpins both cryptocurrencies and NFTs. People might be forced to purchase the NFTs using cryptocurrency on the NFT exchanges. NFTs and cryptocurrencies, on the other hand, are created and used for a variety of objectives. Cryptocurrencies are structured to function similarly to currencies, holding value and allowing you to buy and sell products. Tokens of cryptocurrency are fungible, just like traditional currencies like the dollar. Unlike crypto tokens, NFTs are non-fungible, resulting in one-of-a-type tokens that can also be used to establish ownership and transfer rights to digital assets.

5.6 NFT Interaction Inside the Metaverse

Users can even have full control of their digital products inside the Metaverse, thanks to NFTs. These virtual worlds are built on blockchain technology, which provides immutable

 Cryptocurrency Investing For Beginners

proof of ownership. If you bought a plot of Land within Decentraland, for instance, the Metaverse would usually provide you with proof of verification in the shape of the NFTs, which would have been guaranteed by blockchain.

The NFTs are very important inside the Metaverse for establishing unique areas and enhancing digital social and community interactions. Premium types of NFTs are mainly used to get entry into the digital world's wealthiest and most affluent types of communities, exclusive advantages, staking rewards, and other high-end collectibles. For example, through the Bored Ape Yacht Club & CryptoPunks collections, select users can acquire access to high-quality communities with password-protected material and sometimes even offline gatherings.

5.7 Crypto Interaction Inside the Metaverse

The money of the Metaverse is a cryptocurrency, and each one of the Metaverses indeed has its very own supply of coins. They're utilized to pay for almost everything, from the NFTs to the virtual real estate to avatar shoes. For instance, MANA, Decentraland's native token, can be utilized to sell and buy anything onto the platform.

5.8 Role of Ethereum in Interconnecting the Metaverse, NFT, and the Crypto Tokens

After Bitcoin, Ethereum is the second-largest cryptocurrency by market capitalization. Not only is it a highly regarded coin, but it also serves as a development platform for Metaverse creators. The bulk of tokens, like MANA and SAND, are ERC20 tokens with no own blockchain. To verify transactions and expand their operations, they use Ethereum's network. As a result, while the platforms themselves may have been created on MANA or SAND, Ethereum is used for everything behind the scenes. On OpenSea, the world's largest NFT platform, Ethereum is also the preferred currency. Furthermore, the bulk of NFTs can be acquired directly from a crypto wallet with ETH. These three principles, as well as the host of other developing technologies like dApps and DeFi, are all powered by Ethereum. As a result, it's one of the few Blockchains that can interface with Metaverses, NFTs, and cryptocurrencies.

Conclusion

A cryptocurrency is a type of digital currency that is represented by an encrypted data string. It is monitored and organized via a peer-to-peer network known as a blockchain. In addition, blockchain acts as a secure database for transactions such as purchasing, selling, and transferring. Cryptocurrencies are frequently created using blockchain technology. Blockchain describes how transactions are stored in "blocks" and time-stamped. It's a time-consuming and difficult process, but the final result is a secure digital record of bitcoin transactions that hackers can't alter. A two-factor authentication method is also required for transactions. You may be prompted to provide a login and password to conduct a transaction. Then you may be asked to provide a text message authentication code issued to your own cell phone. Unlike traditional money, cryptocurrencies are decentralized, meaning governments or other financial institutions do not issue them. Cryptocurrencies are produced (and secured) using cryptographic techniques that are maintained and confirmed through the mining process. Transactions are processed and certified by a network of computers or physical hardware like application-specific integrated circuits (ASICs). As a result of this activity, the network's miners are rewarded with bitcoin.

Cryptocurrency Investing For Beginners

Even though security precautions are in place, cryptocurrencies are not immune to hackers. Several high-profile bitcoin thefts have wreaked havoc on the industry. Coincheck was hacked for $534 million, and BitGrail was hijacked for $195 million, making them two of the costliest cryptocurrency attacks of the year. Unlike government-backed money, the value of virtual currencies is purely decided by supply and demand. This can result in huge market movements, with substantial gains or losses for investors. Furthermore, cryptocurrency investments are subject to far less government regulation than traditional financial products such as stocks, bonds, and mutual funds. Before you invest, learn about bitcoin exchanges.

According to data, there are roughly 500 exchanges to select from. Do your research, read reviews, and talk to more experienced investors before selecting. If you buy bitcoin, you must keep it safe. You may store it in a digital wallet or trade it on a cryptocurrency market. While several types of wallets exist, each has its own set of benefits, technological needs, and security features. Just as with exchanges, you should investigate your storage choices before investing. Diversification is a key component of any successful investment plan, and this is especially true in the case of cryptocurrencies. Do not invest all of your money in Bitcoin simply because it is a well-known digital currency. There are dozens of options, and diversifying your portfolio by investing in different digital currencies is good. Be aware that the cryptocurrency market is quite volatile, so expect swings in price. Prices will swing drastically. If your investment portfolio or mental health can't handle it, cryptocurrency may not be a suitable fit for you. Cryptocurrency is all the rage right now, but bear in mind that it is still in its early stages and is considered extremely speculative. Be prepared for the difficulties that come with making a new investment. If you decide to participate, first conduct your research and make a small investment.

BOOKS PUBLISHED BY PHAROS BOOKS

 sales@pharosbooks.in    011-40395855   www.pharosbooks.in

A-55, Main Mother Dairy Road, Pandav Nagar, East Delhi-110092